It's Festival Time . . .

Both pagan and Christian festivals are celebrated with much gaiety in Ireland. Irish festivals are famous for their music, storytelling, games and dressing up. Come get dizzy dancing around a maypole, crown a goat at Puck's Fair or kick up your heels at a gypsy campfire. It's festival time in Ireland . . .

WHERE'S IRELAND?

Ireland is an island in Western Europe. The island is divided into two parts: Northern Ireland, which is part of the United Kingdom, and the Republic of Ireland.

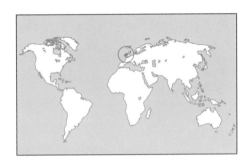

Rain from the Atlantic Ocean blows across the island, making it green both in summer and winter. For this reason, Ireland is often called the 'Emerald Isle'. Along the western coast are mountains, which the Irish call *reeks*. There are also lots of lakes called loughs.

Who are the Irish?

In 450 B.C., **Celts** from Middle Europe moved across the oceans to settle in Ireland. They believed in many gods. They also believed in little people, such as fairies, elves and **leprechauns**.

After the birth of Christ, traders and soldiers arrived from Rome and introduced Christianity to the island.

In the nineteenth century, a disease attacked the potato crops and about one million people starved to death. More than one million Irish left the country to make their homes in England, Scotland, Canada and the United States. They took their customs and beliefs with them. Do you have a friend or neighbour whose ancestors lived in Ireland?

A smiling Irish girl. Look at her lovely red hair!

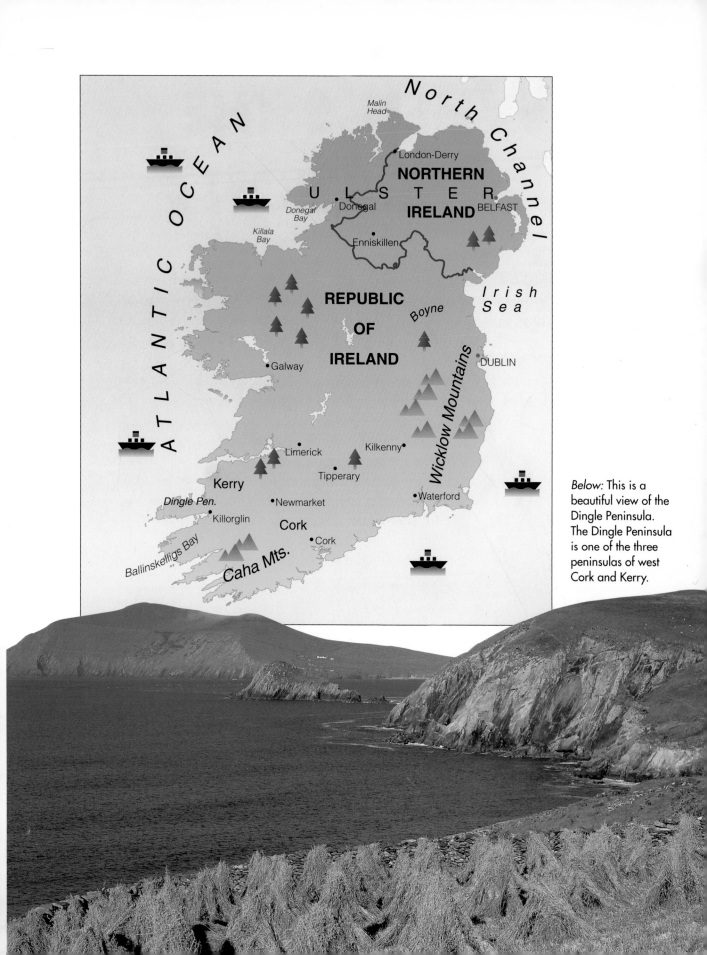

Below: This is a beautiful view of the Dingle Peninsula. The Dingle Peninsula is one of the three peninsulas of west Cork and Kerry.

Map labels:

North Channel

Malin Head

ATLANTIC OCEAN

London-Derry

NORTHERN

U L S T E R

Donegal Bay

Donegal

IRELAND

BELFAST

Killala Bay

Enniskillen

Irish Sea

REPUBLIC

Boyne

OF

Galway

IRELAND

DUBLIN

Wicklow Mountains

Kilkenny

Limerick

Tipperary

Kerry

Waterford

Dingle Pen.

Newmarket

Killorglin

Cork

Ballinskelligs Bay

Cork

Caha Mts.

WHEN'S THE CELEBRATION?

SPRING

✪ **CHALK SUNDAY** (The first Sunday of Lent) – Unmarried people are marked with chalk as they enter the church. Traditionally, Catholics were not allowed to marry during Lent, so they had to wait until after Easter. Marking them with chalk is a way of teasing them for not being married.

✪ **SAINT PATRICK'S DAY**

✪ **EASTER** – At Easter Day dances, a large cake is exhibited for all to see. Men pay to dance and the one who dances the most 'takes the cake'. This expression here refers to a person who dances more than anyone else.

✪ **MAY DAY** – A folk festival that was celebrated before Christianity and is still celebrated with maypole dancing and flower gathering. Bushes are decorated with flowers or eggshells, which are symbols of life. There is plenty of dancing and singing.

Do you like my fairy costume?

SUMMER

✪ **BONFIRE NIGHT** – Originally, animal and human bones were burnt to appease the gods on Bonfire, or Bone Fire, Night. Later, Bonfire Night became a celebration of the eternal flame of Saint Patrick on the shortest night of the year. Now it is celebrated with dancing and storytelling around the fire.

✪ **MIDSUMMER'S EVE** – Watch out for fairies on this night. They are out to steal mortal brides for themselves. All girls should be kept indoors!

✪ **MIDSUMMER'S DAY** – Country fairs are held with dancing and singing.

✪ **ORANGE DAY PARADE**

✪ **LUGHNASA** – Traditionally, the beginning of the harvest was celebrated with festivities dedicated to the pre-Christian god Lugh.

✪ **PUCK'S FAIR**

AUTUMN

⚙ **AUTUMN HARVEST FESTIVAL** – Farmers bring their harvests to town to trade or sell. Potatoes are used to make *poteen*, a drink that is sold at fairs. People get very jolly. There is lots of dancing and singing, music and storytelling.

⚙ **SAMHAIN**

⚙ **NOVEMBER EVE** – A night when fairies are said to appear. The fairies are sad on this night because they open the graves of the dead and dance with ghosts on the graveyard tombstones. They also try to capture a mortal musician to play for them.

Don't you think our maypole looks colourful? Come dance with us!

⚙ **SAINT MARTIN'S DAY** – A Celtic tradition was to kill animals on this day as food for the winter. A little rooster's blood was sprinkled on the doors of houses to keep evil spirits away. Today, farmers put religious medals in all four corners of their fields.

WINTER

⚙ **CHRISTMAS**

⚙ **SAINT STEPHEN'S DAY** – Celtic myth had it that the robin (representing the New Year) killed the wren (representing the Old Year) during this time. Wren Boys blacken their faces and go from house to house asking for money to bury the wren. The money they collect is used to buy food and drink for the 'wren dance' held on this night.

⚙ **SAINT BRIGID'S DAY**

Onward march we go! Come follow us!

SAINT BRIGID'S DAY

I n the old days, 1 February was considered the start of the growth season. After Christianity was introduced, Saint Brigid (Bridie) was honoured instead of the pagan gods. The success of agriculture depended on her help. Thus, her feast day was a special celebration and still is today.

Dandelions in full bloom.

Sold into slavery

This very popular female patron saint of Ireland was a fifth-century nun who is credited with founding the first convent in Ireland.

Brigid had her beginnings as a slave. Born in Ireland, she was sold into slavery by her own father. When she was freed, she returned to her father voluntarily as a serving girl. She milked cows and made butter. She is also said to have woven the first piece of cloth in Ireland and so became the patron saint of weavers and spinners. Even when she became the head of a **monastery**, she kept doing the things she loved best, such as reaping and making butter.

Left: A ewe and two lambs taking a walk.

Opposite: Wearing masks and visiting homes are all part of the celebrations on Saint Brigid's Day.

Stories about Saint Brigid

On Saint Brigid's Day, people cannot work on anything that involves spinning, digging or turning a wheel because 'Saint Brigid's Day is free from twistings'. This way, the feast day can be a holiday for the farmers.

This is Saint Brigid's well. It is a holy place where people pray to Bridie, honouring her. **Rosary beads** or strips of cloth are left there as a remembrance of the visit.

Perhaps Saint Brigid was able to place her foot in water or dip her finger in the brook on 1 February because the first good weather was thought to arrive on this day. As the Irish say, this was the day when 'away went the hen that hatches the cold (winter)'.

Brigid's feast day is associated with the promise of spring, warmth, new grass, lambs and milk. The dandelion is known as the Plant of the Bride (from 'Bridie') because it yields a milky juice believed to have nourished young spring lambs.

'Brigid's Cloak', or *brat bhride*, was a woven cloth left on the doorstep outside on the eve of Brigid's feast day. During the night, the cloth was believed to acquire special healing powers. People would place the cloth around the necks of sick animals to help them get well.

The custom of having women propose marriage to men during a Leap Year can also be traced to Saint Brigid, who persuaded Saint Patrick to grant women that right one year out of every four.

Spinning away at the wheel! Look at how much raw wool there is in the basket!

Feast Day

The Feast Day of Saint Brigid is on 1 February and, in many places in rural Ireland, people still make Brigid Crosses to honour her. Pageants take place at schools and churches with young women carrying green rushes.

On the eve of Saint Brigid's Day, crosses are woven out of rushes and hung for a year above the doors of houses and barns. These crosses are believed to protect the house and the livestock from harm and fire. No evil spirit can pass these charms.

A small folk play is enacted in which a girl playing the part of Brigid brings rushes to the door and is allowed inside. She blesses the family, eats with them and helps them make crosses.

This old picture shows a man making Saint Brigid's crosses from straw. After the making of the crosses on the eve of Saint Brigid's feast day, apple griddle cakes are eaten as a tradition.

PUCK'S FAIR

Every year in August, the people of Killorglin in County Kerry busily prepare for a three-day fair. For hundreds of years, this town has been the centre for a **livestock** fair that has become a major tourist attraction.

Crowning of a billy goat

On Gathering Day when stalls are opened to sell food and drink and booths are opened for trade and **barter**, a large billy goat is decorated with ribbons and paraded through the streets. He is crowned 'King of the Fair' and placed on a three-storey platform (his throne) in the town square, where he presides over the fair for three days!

Opposite (top): Look at the little girl crowning the goat during the procession. According to a tale, when the Killorglin Fair first started, the only animal taken there was a billy goat. It was made the fair's symbol because the townsfolk were so grateful. This 'crowning' then made the fair attractive to other people who traded in animals.

Left: Look at these two girls enjoying a pony ride at Puck's Fair in Killorglin. Have you ever ridden a pony?

12

Stories about King Puck

Many people believe the goat is the most perceptive of all animals and that it can even see the wind. That is why the goat is king of the fair.

Hundreds of years ago when the Normans held goat fairs, or puck fairs, a goat was 'enthroned' to show that the market was in progress. The popular explanation given for the origin of the Killorglin fair is that English soldiers **plundered** the area long ago. Seeing this happen, a billy goat collected all the farm animals and led them up a mountain to safety. He was crowned king of the fair to honour his bravery.

Here are two boys resting on the dodgems. These are small electric cars found at fairs. Driving in an enclosed area, you can either knock into somebody or move away.

It takes a powerful pair
of lungs to make music
at the fair!

Campfire music

Another name for the gypsies is Travellers. Their homes
are gaily coloured caravans or wagons, and they travel from
place to place. At Killorglin, they camp the caravans along
the road. At night, they light great campfires and play Irish
music. You can hear reels, **jigs**, hornpipes, airs, marches and
old Irish waltzes.

Both people and animals enjoy a sunny day at Puck's Fair.

Gypsies join in

The second day of the fair features a livestock show. Gypsies in large numbers have attended this fair for hundreds of years. They sell and trade horses, donkeys, wagons and carts.

Scattering Day

Wouldn't you like to go for a ride in this horse-drawn carriage, too?

On the evening of the third day, King Puck is led out of town by a piper to the accompaniment of traditional Irish music. This signifies the end of the fair.

Think about this

Puck comes from Old English and means mischievous **sprite**, goblin or elf. It is also a word for the devil. The hair from a goat's whiskers or a goat's foot is believed to drive away evil spirits.

SAINT PATRICK'S DAY

Every year on 17 March, the Irish people honour their patron saint, Patrick, who is also known as Saint Pat or Paddy. His symbol is a shamrock, so the Irish wear shamrocks on his day. They attend special religious services and have community and family gatherings as well. Colourful parades pass through towns and cities led by brass and pipe bands.

Kidnapped by pirates

When Paddy was a young boy of 16, he lived in the British countryside. Pirates from across the Irish Sea kidnapped him, brought him to Erin (Ireland's poetic name) and sold him as a slave. For six years, he was a shepherd in the mountains. Finally, he escaped and went to a monastery in Europe, where he trained to become a priest in the Roman Catholic Church. After many years, he became a bishop and, in A.D. 432, when he was about 60 years old, he returned to Erin to be a missionary to the pagan Celts. He spent the rest of his life doing missionary work.

The shamrock belongs to the clover family of plants. Look at the shamrocks painted on the faces of this happy pair!

Left: This man is dressed as Saint Patrick. The real Saint Patrick is credited with bringing the warm weather for planting, otherwise known as 'turning up the warm side of the stone'.

Below: A smiling girl enjoys herself. See how warmly she is bundled up.

Miracle man

Ireland was a wild place until Saint Patrick arrived. He travelled the country teaching Christianity and converting the pagans. He gradually changed the pagan festivals into Holy Days and created many holy places for people to worship God. He built monasteries and churches. He also performed many good and charitable works and even a few miracles!

The shamrock

The shamrock is a small, three-leafed plant that appears in the middle of a season the Celts called Growth. Patrick used the three leaves on one stem to explain the **Holy Trinity** (three persons in one God) to the Celtic tribes.

Legends about Saint Patrick

One tale about Saint Patrick involves a family who refused to be hospitable to him when he appeared at their door. They sent him to the stable to sleep. The next morning, all that remained of the house and its occupants was a hole in the ground! Patrick was annoyed at his mistreatment and caused the house and its family to disappear. Perhaps this is why the Irish people are known today for their hospitality.

Top: These smiling faces show the fun and excitement of celebrating Saint Patrick's Day!

Left: How long do you think it takes to paint a shamrock on your forehead?

Saint Pat's celebration

People all over the world celebrate Saint Patrick's Day on 17 March. In Ireland, there are parades during the day and special dinners at night of corned beef and cabbage, traditional Irish fare. People wear green clothing, badges, buttons or ribbons on that day because green is the colour of the shamrock and the Emerald Isle. This custom is called the wearing of the green. Some people even drink beer that has been dyed green with food colouring. It is also a tradition to have a drink of Patrick's Pot (whisky) on his feast day. Years ago, people put a sprig of shamrock in their whisky; this way, they could 'drown the shamrock'.

In the evening, people meet up in neighbourhood pubs to eat and drink, sing Irish folk songs, dance Irish jigs and tell stories and legends.

Think about this

The largest parade in Ireland to celebrate Saint Patrick takes place in Dublin, but the biggest parade of all is held in New York City. It dates back to 1762. Boston has an even older parade that started in 1737. Can you imagine why this would be?

The largest parade in Ireland – Saint Patrick's Day in Dublin. Huge crowds gather to see the floats and bands.

SAMHAIN

On 31 October, children dress up in costumes, wear masks and carry lanterns from house to house to receive treats or play tricks. The lanterns are often carved out of turnips, with scary faces and candles inside. Pumpkin lanterns are also popular.

Below: Adults seem to enjoy dressing up in costumes as much as the children do! Can you identify the character each adult is dressed up as?

Ghosts and goblins

Samhain was the Celtic New Year. This festival began when the Celts lived in Ireland and honoured Saman, the Lord of the Dead. They believed that the souls of people who had died the year before gathered at this time. Being greatly fearful, they used magic to lay evil spirits to rest. People thought the evil spirits would grab anyone found roaming after dark, so they carried fiery torches and disguised themselves with masks and costumes.

The saints come marching in

In 834, Pope Gregory IV made Samhain into a church festival honouring all saints. It was called Hallowmas. All Saint's Day fell on 1 November, so 31 October was All Hallow's Eve, which eventually became Halloween.

Opposite: To the Celts, 'The Fires of Peace' occurred when people carried fire torches and went to houses to rid them of evil spirits. Here, the crowd enjoys a different type of fire.

Snapping at apples

Children call this festival Snap Apple Night because they save the best apples from the harvest for games such as bobbing for apples, spearing apples in tubs of water and trying to bite apples swinging from the rafters by strings. Hazelnuts, which the Celts associated with knowledge and which were used in fortune-telling, are collected from trees, cracked and eaten on this night. A popular dish served during this festival is *boxty*, which resembles a pancake and is made from potatoes.

Above: Bobbing for apples can be a lot of fun but it is a lot harder than it looks!

Right: This little girl is trying to eat an apple on a string during Halloween. Do you like apples?

Fancy dress and fireworks

For children today, Halloween is a time for fancy dress parties and fireworks. It is also an opportunity for friends and relatives to get together for a meal and perhaps some playful fortune-telling. Traditional dishes are apple tart and *barmbrack*, a type of fruit loaf.

Wow! Have you ever seen a mask this big? How heavy do you think it is?

Think about this
Myths are much more than just make-believe tales. They are the remnants of ideas humans once lived by. Many old myths survive as festivals for young people. Halloween is an example.

23

ORANGE DAY

If you are a Protestant living in Northern Ireland, you probably have a friend or relative who is a member of the Orange Society. Each year on 12 July, the Orangemen hold a parade. People gather to listen to religious and political speeches.

Orange lilies

Orange Day is the anniversary of the Battle of the Boyne, which took place in Ireland in July 1690. The trouble began when James II, a Roman Catholic king, lost his throne to William of Orange, who was a Protestant. Each side raised an army of about 30,000 men, and they fought on the banks of the Boyne River. The Protestants won the battle but the Catholics formed '**underground societies**' to restore the line of James. The Protestants formed the Orange Order to maintain links with England. William of Orange became a hero to all Protestants.

Orangemen abroad

The Loyal Orange Institute was organised in 1795 in Ulster, a region in Northern Ireland. Orangemen support Protestant Christianity and civil and religious freedom. They meet regularly in groups called **lodges**. Many Irish Protestants who have moved away from Ireland have set up lodges in their new countries – mainly England, Scotland, Canada, and the United States – and still celebrate Orange Day on 12 July.

Left: This is what William of Orange looked like. When he fought in battle, he wore a spray of orange lilies as his symbol. Today, the orange lily remains his symbol.

Opposite: The Orange Day Parade in Belfast. Besides having orange lilies pinned to their clothing, the marchers also wear orange sashes. They march to stirring music and carry banners.

THINGS FOR YOU TO DO

Do you wonder what Gaelic sounds like? Here is your chance to find out! Try learning how to say the days of the week and some numbers in Gaelic.

Speak Gaelic

The Celts' language has lasted for 2,000 years in Ireland. Today, Irish people speak English and Gaelic, the language handed down from the Celts. Here are some words you can practise. If you meet someone from Ireland, you can surprise him or her by speaking Gaelic.

Days of the week

Monday	*Luan [LOO-in]*
Tuesday	*Mairt [MARTCH]*
Wednesday	*Ceadaoin [KAY-deen]*
Thursday	*Deardaoin [JEYR-deen]*
Friday	*Aoine [HAYN-ya]*
Saturday	*Sathairn [sa-HARN]*
Sunday	*Domhnach [DOW-neg]*

Numbers

One	*Aon [AYN]*
Two	*Do [DAU]*
Three	*Tri [TREE]*
Four	*Ceathar [KE-har]*
Five	*Cuig [KOO-ig]*
Six	*Se [SHAY]*
Seven	*Seacht [SHAKT]*
Eight	*Ocht [OKHT]*
Nine	*Naci [NEE]*
Ten	*Deich [JEYKH]*

Exercise your vocal cords!

Do you enjoy music? Here is a short song for you to sing. If you have a friend who plays the piano or the guitar, you can try out this song together. You might even want to perform this piece for your family after dinner!

Cut the Loaf

When I was young I had no sense, I bought a wee fid-dle for eigh-teen pence, And all the tune that I could play was cut the loaf and ate a-way.

Further information

www.puckfair.ie/ — the official website of Puck's Fair with lots of background information

www.new-age.co.uk/celtic-festivals-samhain.htm — lots of fascinating information about Samhain traditions

www.st-patricks-day.com/index.asp — links to more information about the history and culture of St Patrick's Day

www.grandorange.org.uk/history/King_William_Ulster.html — background history of Orange Day

Every effort has been made by the Publisher to ensure that these websites are suitable for children and contain no inappropriate or offensive material. However, because of the nature of the Internet, it is impossible to guarantee that the contents of these sites will not be altered. We strongly advise that Internet access is supervised by a responsible adult.

MAKE A SHAMROCK NECKLACE

M ake your own shamrock to wear on Saint Patrick's Day. The shamrock is the symbol for Ireland. The green is the colour of the beautiful Emerald Isle.

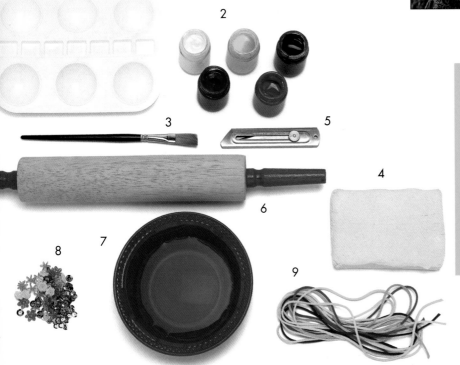

1

2

3

5

6

4

7

8

9

You will need:
1. A paint tray
2. Paints of different colours
3. A paintbrush
4. Some modelling clay
5. A paper cutter
6. A rolling pin
7. A bowl of water
8. Sequins
9. Threads of different colours.

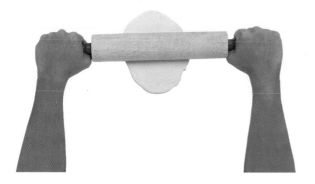

1 Flatten the clay using the rolling pin.

2 Cut out the shape of a shamrock with your paper cutter. Poke a hole at the top of your clay shamrock with the end of your paintbrush.

3 Wait for the clay to dry. Paint the shamrock any colour you want and wait for that to dry.

4 Decorate your clay shamrock with sequins. Pull a piece of thread through the hole on the shamrock and tie the ends together.

MAKE SHAMROCK BISCUITS

The Irish people grow lots of potatoes, and many Irish recipes include them. They are a staple of the Irish diet. These biscuits will help you and your family celebrate Saint Patrick's Day. If you like nuts and raisins, you can add a half cup (60 g) of each to the biscuit batter.

You will need:

1. 300 g hot, cooked potatoes
2. 100 g sugar
3. 60 ml honey
4. 200 g butter or margarine
5. 140 g all-purpose flour
6. 2 teaspoons baking powder
7. 1 teaspoon ground cinnamon or ground allspice
8. $1/4$ teaspoon ground cloves
9. $1/2$ teaspoon grated nutmeg
10. $1/2$ teaspoon salt
11. 1 egg for brushing
12. Green sprinkles
13. A large bowl
14. A wooden spoon
15. Measuring spoons
16. Measuring cups
17. A sieve
18. An oven glove
19. A pastry brush
20. A baking tray
21. A teaspoon
22. A potato masher

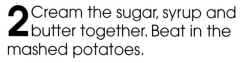

1 Place the hot, cooked potatoes in a large bowl and mash them thoroughly.

2 Cream the sugar, syrup and butter together. Beat in the mashed potatoes.

3 Sift together the flour, baking powder, spices and salt. Add the sifted, dry ingredients to the mixture to make a dough. Mix until it is smooth.

4 Using a teaspoon, drop three small mounds of dough close together to form the shape of a shamrock on a lightly greased baking tray.

5 Brush the tops of the biscuits with some lightly beaten egg. Top with green sprinkles and bake for 20 minutes at 190° Celsius (gas mark 5). This recipe makes 40 biscuits or more, so you can invite your friends over to share them.

GLOSSARY

barter, 12   To trade or exchange one object for another.

Celts, 4   The early settlers in Ireland who arrived before Christianity.

Holy Trinity, 17   The Christian belief of Father, Son and Holy Spirit as three beings in one God.

jig, 14   The music that goes along with a folk dance that is characterised by kicking and leaping.

leprechaun, 4   A mischievous elf in Irish folklore, sometimes called the elves' shoemaker.

livestock, 12   Animals such as horses and sheep that are kept on a farm.

lodge, 24   The meeting place and members of a group of men with the same interests, such as the Orangemen.

monastery, 8   A place where people who join religious orders live and work.

plunder, 13   To steal or loot, as pirates do, or as in a war.

rosary beads, 10   A string of beads that Roman Catholics count when they pray.

sprite, 15   An elf or fairy.

underground society, 24   A group of people who meet secretly.

INDEX

Picture credits
Abbie Enock: 15 (bottom); Sylvia Cordaiy Photo Library Ltd: 3 (top); Haga Library, Japan: 17 (bottom), 18 (both);Hoaqui: 9; Renata Holzbachová/ Philippe Bénet: 7 (bottom); Life File: 8 (bottom); Northern Ireland Tourist Board: 4, 10 (bottom), 28; David Simson: 12, 13 (both), 14; The Slide File: cover, 2, 5, 6, 7 (top), 10 (top), 15 (top), 16, 17 (top), 19, 20 (bottom), 21, 22 (bottom), 23, 25; J. J. Sommeryns/ A.N.A. Press Agency: 24; Topham Picture Point: 1, 3 (bottom), 8 (top), 20 (top), 22 (top); Ulster Folk & Transport Museum: 11 (WAG 1965)